ATLANTA

A PICTURE BOOK TO REMEMBER HER BY

Designed by
DAVID GIBBON

Produced by
TED SMART

CRESCENT

INTRODUCTION

In 1837, a civil engineer named Stephen Long, employed to survey the best route for the Georgia State Railroad, commented that the collection of shacks known as the 'Terminus' would be "a good location for one tavern, a blacksmith shop, a grocery store and nothing else". From such humble beginnings, however, has emerged one of the nation's leading cities, Atlanta, a city whose economic growth still depends to a great extent on transportation; a city that has become the rail, air and communications centre of the entire South-East.

In the early part of the 19th century much of America was in the grip of railroad fever and Georgia was no exception. The area chosen for the terminal of the Western and Atlantic Railroad was virgin forest that had only recently been ceded to the State by the Creek Indian Nation. Nearby was a staging inn known as the White Hall and there were also a few small farms. As the 'Terminus' started to expand it was renamed Marthasville, after the daughter of former Governor Wilson Lumpkin, a great advocate of the railroad system. This name, however, did not last for long as J. Edgar Thompson, Chief Engineer of the Georgia Railroad, began listing the station as Atlanta – a feminine form of the 'Atlantic' in Western and Atlantic. As all the incoming rail freight was marked in this way, so the name Marthasville was discarded and in 1847 the Legislature granted Atlanta a municipal charter.

Gradually, more rail lines were completed which linked with Atlanta, turning it into an important junction. As a consequence the town began to grow; hotels and warehouses were built and the wholesale and distribution of goods became vitally important.

By the 1860's access to Atlanta was so good that it became the supply and communication centre for the Confederacy. Alas, in 1864 Civil War arrived. Three battles were fought: the Battle of Peachtree Creek, the Battle of Atlanta and the Battle of Ezra Church. On September 2nd of 1864, after a protracted siege, the Mayor formally surrendered to the Union Army under the command of William T. Sherman. In November, as he moved out on his devastating March to the Sea, General Sherman ordered that Atlanta be burned. All but four hundred of the four thousand five hundred houses and commercial buildings were destroyed and the rail facilities demolished.

The citizens who remained were determined to rebuild the city as one more beautiful than before; a city that would rise out of the ashes like a phoenix. This mythical bird, the symbol of resurrected life, is depicted on the city's official seal. Four years after the war the city was designated State Capital of Georgia and reconstruction began in earnest.

Today, Atlanta has the country's second busiest airport and the city's accessibility by rail and road has made it an important industrial centre, particularly for the aircraft, automobile, iron and steel and textile industries. It is also the national headquarters for many of America's leading companies.

In the 1960's and 70's, new buildings have rapidly replaced old, especially in the Downtown area. Hotels of futuristic design, a World Congress Centre with a vast exhibition area, simultaneous interpretation facilities for six languages and, of course, shops and restaurants, have led to the city's position of importance as a national and international convention centre.

Other impressive modern buildings include the Omni International Megastructure, a complete entertainments complex with exclusive shops, cinemas, restaurants, a hotel and an ice-skating rink, all contained under a climate-controlled, fourteen-storey high plastic roof.

In 1965 the Atlanta Stadium was completed with a seating capacity of 58,000. It is the venue for all manner of sports including basketball, baseball, football and the increasingly popular game of soccer.

The Memorial Arts Centre caters culturally for all tastes in its presentation of art, ballet, music, opera and repertory theatre.

To many people around the world, the name Margaret Mitchell, the author of that remarkable tale of the Civil War, 'Gone With the Wind', is synonymous with the city. Begun in 1926 and winner of the Pullitzer Prize for fiction in 1937, the book was also made into a film that proved to be a cinema classic and it is still shown to audiences in numerous countries. Margaret Mitchell is buried in Oakland Cemetery, in the south-east of the city, along with several thousand victims of the Civil War of which she wrote.

Also in Atlanta is Tullie Smith's House. Built in 1840, it is one of the few pre-Civil War houses still standing in this area. It was donated to the city's Historical Society by Tullie Smith's descendants and has been carefully restored. Here the visitor may see the lifestyle of a yeoman farmer in Piedmont Georgia in the mid-19th century. With 810 acres of land and eleven slaves, the Smith's of that time lived off the land, working hard each day from dawn to dusk. Contrary to popular belief, there was only a small minority of Southerners who owned grand mansions and scores of slaves and who could, therefore, afford to sit back and watch the work being done.

Returning to the heart of Atlanta, the skyline is very much dominated by soaring skyscrapers and yet at one time the Capitol, with its glittering dome of gold from the Georgia Hills, was the tallest building in the area.

Not far away from the Capitol is another monument, the marble tomb of Dr Martin Luther King, which stands near the Ebenezer Baptist Church where he was co-pastor with his father. The most memorable speech made by this gifted man began: "I had a dream…" His dream, of course, was the realisation of racial harmony.

To the Civil War survivors of the Battle of Atlanta, their dream was to see their city live again. This dream has certainly been fulfilled, and perhaps in time the hopes of another great citizen of Atlanta will reach fruition.

Symbolising the remarkable growth and spirit of Atlanta is the magnificent bronze statue of the Phoenix *left*.

Hartsfield International Airport *above* and *above left* is the country's second busiest airport and is still expanding rapidly to accommodate Atlanta's busy traffic flow.

One of the city's fire engines is shown *left*, whilst *below left* a group of visitors pose for a photograph outside the Atlanta Hilton Hotel.

The interesting character *below,* on his decorated bicycle, provides an amusing sight on one of Atlanta's streets.

Although no longer Atlanta's tallest building, the State Capitol with it's gold dome *right*, is nevertheless its most distinctive. In the foreground is a replica of the Statue of Liberty, presented by the Boy Scouts.

Atlanta's skyline *overleaf* is especially exciting when seen by night. This view shows the downtown area, with its skyscraper hotels and office blocks, surrounding the floodlit State Capitol.

Less than 150 years ago Atlanta was merely a terminal point for a new railroad. With rapid expansion, however, the city has become the transportation hub of the southeastern states of the U.S.A.

One of Atlanta's many freight trains is featured *above*, whilst *left* and *above left* can be seen the busy freeways, which together with the rail and air links are the very mainstay of Atlanta's existence.

Part of the Metropolitan Atlanta Rapid Transit Authority's (MARTA) construction programme is shown *below*. This particular rail system provides fast transit service to two major metropolitan counties, De Kalb and Fulton, and its large fleet of city buses ensures optimum efficiency.

Atlanta's skyline *right* provokes interest from any angle.

One of the most ambitious schemes to be carried out in the city is the vast Omni complex.

This unique centre includes the Georgia World Congress Centre and the Omni International Hotel which can be seen in the superb aerial view *below right.*

The plastic roof of the Megastructure, part of which is shown *above,* covers 14 storeys, and the complex features various shops *centre right,* restaurants and cinemas, as well as the magnificent skating rink *left, top right, below* and *overleaf.*

Atlanta's hotels and restaurants are noted for their exciting and sophisticated cuisine, and to complete the night's entertainment offer a wide variety of cabarets, which often feature international stars.

Every taste is catered for and includes jazz, folk-singing and even the French can-can. After dining on exquisitely prepared food the guest can relax and enjoy the floorshows in plush and elegant surroundings: thus making his visit to Atlanta an occasion to be remembered.

Timeless fountains *right* play in the foreground against the 20th century backdrop of the city's skyline.

Fabulous panoramas of the city can be seen from the Colony Square Hotel's highest restaurant *above*, whilst at one of the cafés in the Colony Square Complex *above left* guests enjoy a quiet drink.

One of Atlanta's famous landmarks and reputed to be the world's tallest hotel, is the Peachtree Plaza. It boasts a half-acre lake in the lobby *left* and *overleaf* and a slowly revolving restaurant at the top of the building. Entertainment *below* is also of the highest standard.

Another fine example of modern architecture is the Atlanta Hilton Hotel *above*, one of the newest hotels in the city.

Skilfully designed by John Portman, the Peachtree Centre *left*, is a magnificent complex which is virtually a city within a city and is sited in downtown Atlanta.

The spectacular lobby of the Regency Hyatt Hotel is shown *right*. This impressive hotel contains 1,000 rooms and towers twenty-three storeys high. The glass-enclosed high-speed elevators are a particular feature of the hotel.

The Marriot Hotel featured in the two photographs *overleaf* shows the cool, sun-dappled patio with its tempting swimming pool. The Marriot is just one of Atlanta's superb hotels which offer a wide variety of facilities to the city's many visitors.

The circular Peachtree Hotel *above* and *left*, within the Peachtree Complex *overleaf*, is a familiar part of the city's skyline.

John Portman, the designer, conceived the idea of using a tall, tube-like tower, the base of which was contained within a low podium, in order to obtain the maximum amount of air space from the minimum of floor space. The circular tower, coated in bronze glass oblongs, is only 116 feet in diameter yet provides a total of 1,070 rooms. The unique charm of the Peachtree Plaza is sure to appeal to all visitors.

The dazzling car lights illuminate the busy freeways *right*.

Underground Atlanta – Atlanta's newest area of night-life – with its old shops, cobbled streets and gas lamps, has been skilfully restored to resemble its original state at the turn of the century.

Some seventy years ago it was deemed necessary to build a series of viaducts over the railroad tracks to allow the already growing volume of traffic to flow unimpeded across the city centre; this resulted in the desertion of the area at ground level.

Now that the area has once more been brought to life, the many restaurants, such as 'Dante's Down the Hatch', renowned for its fondues, attract many visitors with their nostalgic appeal.

Anthony's Restaurant *overleaf* is set in a beautiful antebellum mansion and is a delightful place in which to eat.

Two of Atlanta's oldest buildings are the City Hall *above left*, and the Judicial *above*; the latter housing the Supreme Court and the Court of Appeal.

The bronze statue of the Phoenix *right* perpetuates the 'Spirit of Atlanta', the city which 'rose again from the ashes'.

The statue *below left* commemorates Henry W. Grady, who, when editor of the Atlanta Constitution, inspired the people with his call for the emergence of the South. The statue looks out over one of the nation's busiest financial districts and is a fitting tribute to his great foresight.

Atlanta's freeways *overleaf* weave in and out of the city as shown in this most effective aerial night shot.

Crowned with gold from the Georgia Hills, the State Capitol *left* stands resplendent against a blue sky, whilst *above right* is shown part of the interior.

A bust of James Edward Oglethorpe, first Resident Trustee of Georgia, is displayed inside the Capitol *above*, and the university *right* is named in his honour.

Georgia State University is shown *below* and *overleaf* can be seen part of Atlanta University.

Nightfall over Atlanta brings a particular splendour to this exciting city.

The statue of 'Miss Freedom', with torch held aloft, crowns the beautifully floodlit State Capitol Building *right*. Modelled on the nation's Capitol in Washington, Georgia's Capitol displays a dome of gold which was brought from Dahlonega, and the building was dedicated in 1889.

Blending successfully with the modern skyscrapers of the downtown area, the lovely Capitol building can be seen again *left*.

John Portman's magnificent Peachtree Centre Complex *above* enhances Atlanta's fascinating skyline.

Piedmont Park *above left,* where concerts are frequently performed, is one of Atlanta's many lovely parks, and the City Park pictured *below left* is yet another.

Atlanta is the home of 'Coca-Cola', the world famous drink, which was created here in 1886. The Coca-Cola Building and Museum *above* contains some fascinating exhibits, of which the barrel shown *right* is just one particular example.

The Memorial Arts Centre *below* is the city's hub of music, opera and ballet. It was dedicated to the members of the Atlanta Arts Association who lost their lives in the plane crash at Orly Airport, Paris, in 1962.

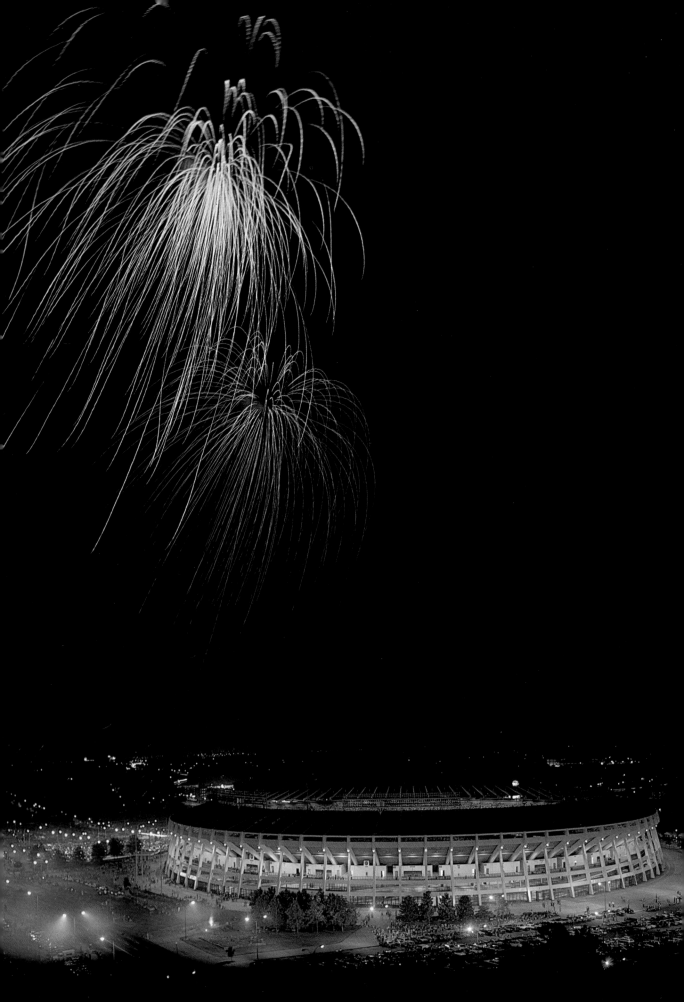

Firework displays are a perennial attraction and this particular dazzling display emanates from the imposing Atlanta Stadium as part of the celebrations commemorating the 4th July.

The colourful and exciting 4th July Parade dominates Atlanta's normally busy streets, *these pages* and *overleaf*, and the Mayor, Maynard Jackson, with his wife, *above*, wave enthusiastically to the many people participating in the celebrations.

The magnificent Atlanta Stadium featured on *these pages* and *overleaf* was completed in 1965, and it is here that Atlanta's professional baseball and football teams, the Braves and the Falcons, delight the crowds.

Atlantans are enthusiastic spectators and participants in many sports, including soccer, tennis, golf and stock car racing.

The Hawks, Atlanta's basketball team, use the famous Omni Stadium, as do the ice-hockey team, the Flames.

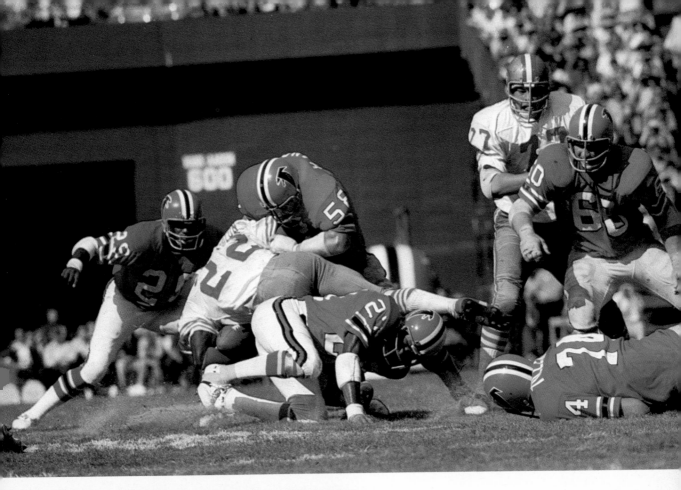

The Falcons, in their distinctive red and white strip, can be seen here in an action-packed football game at the Atlanta Stadium.

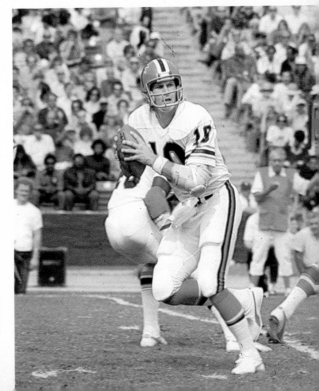

One of Atlanta's most distinguished citizens was the late Dr Martin Luther King Jnr, whose marble tomb *left* and *below* stands as a reminder of his great contribution to the world peace movement.

Father Thomas O'Reilly, pastor of the Church of the Immaculate Conception, is remembered for his great efforts in saving not only his own church, but also the Central Presbyterian Church *above right* and *below right,* from destruction in 1864, during the Civil War. Immaculate Conception was later replaced by the stone and brick building shown *above.*

Tullie Smith's House *above left* typifies a 'plantation plain style' home that was prevalent in Colonial America until after the Civil War. Several similar buildings, including the one shown *above* have been carefully restored by the Atlanta Historical Society, and *overleaf* are pictured some further examples of these lovely mansions, including historic Swan House *right*.

President Jimmy Carter is one of the most famous residents of the splendid Governor's Mansion *above right*, with its 30 columns and 30 rooms, and the beautiful house shown *below right* is Buckhead Mansion.

Like many other states Georgia too had its 'Gold Rush', and places like Auraria *below* and *below left* are now merely ghost-town reminders of that extraordinary era.

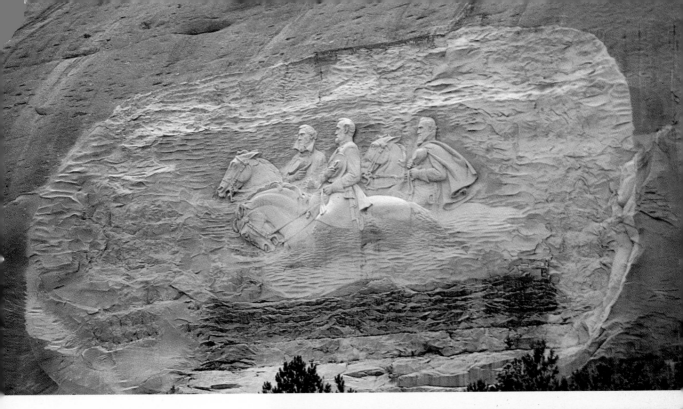

Stone Mountain Park, a few miles outside Atlanta, contains many attractions: the lake *below*, the old covered wooden bridge *centre right*, the 18th Century Grist Mill *left*, and the antebellum Plantation House *below right* with its superb collection of 19th Century antiques.

Not the least of the attractions is the incredible granite carving on the face of Stone Mountain, depicting the Confederate heroes President Jefferson Davies, General Stonewall Jackson and General Robert E. Lee.

Peachtree Centre, world famous for its architecture and sculpture is pictured *overleaf*.

First published in Great Britain 1979 by Colour Library International Ltd.
© Illustrations: Colour Library International Ltd. Colour separations by La Cromolito, Milan, Italy.
Display and text filmsetting by Focus Photoset, London, England.
Printed and bound by L.E.G.O. Vicenza, Italy.
Published by Crescent Books, a division of Crown Publishers Inc.
Library of Congress Catalogue Card No. 78-68675
CRESCENT 1979